Zoo & Cathedral

Zoo & Cathedral

Poems by
Nancy·Johnson

WHITE PINE PRESS • FREDONIA, NEW YORK

Acknowledgements:
Epigraph from Inna Lisnyanskaya from *Metropol: Literary Almanac* by Vasily Aksyonov, Viktor Yerofeyev, et al, eds. Copyright ©1982 by ARDIS/RLT. Copyright ©1979 by Metropol. Reprinted by permission of W.W. Norton & Company, Inc.

Epigraph by Leonard Cohen from "Hallelujah" written by Leonard Cohen ©1995 Bad Monk Publishing. All rights reserved, used by permission.

Grateful acknowledgement is made to the editors of the following magazines in which these poems first appeared:

Another Chicago Magazine: "Suite for Three Left Hands"
Antietam Review: "From a Hospital Bed Downtown"
Antioch Review: "Nationalism"
Apalachee Quarterly: "Meat Counter in Winter"
Carolina Quarterly: "Audience"
College English: "Pastoral"
Gulf Coast: "Sparkman and Water"
Massachusetts Review: "Shopping: The Lipstick Channel"
Monocacy Valley Review: "Ammonite: Hematized Morocco,"
"Morning," "Bryce Canyon"
ONTHEBUS: "Dear Mary"
Puerto Del Sol: "Sopron, Hungary"
Willow Springs: "To a White Crow"

I wish to thank the Pennsylvania Council on the Arts for a grant which allowed me to complete several of these poems.

Book Design: Elaine LaMattina

ISBN 1-877727-58-X

Manufactured in the United States of America

9 8 7 6 5 4 3 2 1

Published by White Pine Press
10 Village Square • Fredonia, New York 14063

For Arthur and the two Wallys

CONTENTS

ZOO & CATHEDRAL

Time and I, we're so alike!
We look like twins.
How can you tell us apart, God?
So, tell me, aren't the escort
And the fugitive
One and the same?

　　　　　　　　　　　—Inna Lisnyanskaya

I

PACKING UP

Yellow Light

Fully formed, your life arrives a dog
ashamed of its nature. You wonder
when it will turn on you and how.

On the road 19 hours from Arkansas
guided by a bruised moon hanging
over D.C. At two in the morning
the last century of miles wakes the runner up,
the ants on your legs, dog in the back seat.

Only the moon and the driver
moving into a yellow tunnel of light,
driving back into the womb, which
no matter how your mother turned out
later, is where you want to be now,
free from future and past.

In the city at 3:30 and out of gas
like so many other nights—
so much saying this is where you
are now. Still shaking, afraid
at every stop light you'll be dry
and have to step into time with a tall
white dog to get home.

IN THE CHAPEL OF THE SUFFERING SAVIOR

He is wearing a red robe, the suffering savior,
that looks like a dress I grew up in except
the robe is tied at the waist with rope. All I know
for sure is: the man died leaving four children
and a wife who bought expensive puzzles. Candles
bank him on both sides, the mirror, the mission,
bleached white. Very bad taste
the bedroom painted red. He was always like that
before things started to happen
in the house. Pinned to Saint Francis Xavier,
who has been reclining incorrupt for years,
are small requests for the favor of life.

First the poodle ate his teeth and then
the doctors took his leg. (Lightning strikes
horizontally.) The neighbors alternated feeding him
dinner and insulin. He recalled his initial attack
and the hospital where they thought he was only drunk
not in shock. His family prayed for his recovery
and to ease the pain taped his picture to Saint Francis.

Which one of them savored hot peppers
I can't be sure. Following his death
the wife married his best friend and they all moved
to Santa Barbara. He'd cut down every Rose of Sharon
even though they were his favorite. Plant one
plant a thousand. And if the dogs were ever chained,
I don't want to know. Old men snort back mucous,
leaves are lying on tables, each moment creaks.

Saints make no sound, although I listen tightly in the night.
He started to eat soup and felt relief
that he wouldn't be there when the dogs discovered
his absence. It's not the kind of question to ask,
but did he die at home? Flames gesture to suffering
as the monsoon whips draperies into the faces of the blessed
and supplicant alike. On the street
the eaten bench and brisk millionaires.

PORCELAIN COOL

If a man throws a knife at you once
he can do it again. It doesn't have to be
the same man, it's enough to know
it can happen. He appears—
brown eyes, beard, straight teeth,
a knife in his hand you know
is coming your way. Consider this
the next time you unwrap your body
and step cleanly. The boy wearing
a yellow inner tube notices
the woman next door. A painter,
she says her life has turned
store brand. She sleeps on a bed
the size of a cracker.
A man is beaten in the parking lot.
You watch him double under punches,
arms slap his lapels. He ducks,
you slip beneath the thin line of the blade
just before it pierces the window
and opens the glass to let in
street light and snow.
The boy jots a note to send himself
a telegram about this when he gets older.
It's the first time and you plan
to go all the way.
Turn up the emotional volume.

AUDIENCE

Here in the midst of green that bores back into my eyes
and texturizes the air, I think of nothing but you
who I am unsure of.
I stroll the lakeside looking for men
too young to know the answers to any questions,
too young to tell me why the luna moth.
Go outside and call my name, yell
so I can detect which way the wind is blowing.
I am the scurry of field mice who sense change,
the crackling of fast movement.
Imagine this—your name on the dry wind.

DOOR TO THE RIVER

In all its pale yellow and browness invites
you through viscous texture called this moment.
What choices will you make on the river's crusty bank?
Different. For instance, here the cruise ship docks
on the 14th floor and someone fiddles
with your keys.

                 A man on the beach
eats pasta salad and spiced shrimp. His birthday
and he massages his bald spot, the woman
at the next blanket with his eyes.
To ignore his dreams he has purchased a dog,
yellow lab to carry a frisbee into the current.

                 Resisting the form of memory
a mannequin rises from the river. She is armless
in gray shadow. Her breasts are finely cracked,
her lips perfect red. She advises you to seek the rehab
center for embroidered voices. You dimple the surface
with a kiss. Swim in, swim out.

Oranges whisper *love resides in water.* On salmon
sand lovers touch shoulders, increase contact
until they are hurling themselves at each other.
Finished in an hour, they ignore
the clean slices of your speech
explaining the need to explain.

                 Handsome flame,
you rise up as morning, willing to forget anything
except the way her fingers wrap your hair,
the river flowing from the mannequin.

The door opens, its dream of dancers billowing
like ocher shirts worn thin. Where you stand
tiny fish curl around your toes and you see
yourself outside the frame, in a gallery
imagining what lies through the door.

                              A German tourist steps
in front of you, interrupting your line of vision,
a woman in Phoenix changes her mind—events
threaded into your life. Inside the painting
you sigh and consider protective
the field of a small universe.

HOUSE ON FIRE

Birds and vegetables are lighting up
the house: a carrot on the lintel,
flamingos on the roof. All done
to give me living space, a place to breathe.

Whose sin was I paying for? My mother
yanked out so much of my hair that by ten
my appearance was tufted. Hair sprouted
from my scalp in sections like a wild garden.

Instead I thought of myself as crested
and noisy as if someone were sitting inside
listening to chunks of ice fall off the roof.
This once was a blue house with shutters.

She pulled with such force that my body
snapped, and as I fell, always slowly,
her mouth set into a thin red line.
I watched her release my hair.

It fell slowly too. When it melted
I was taken by surprise. Like strands of
thinnest parchment, in flickers it was gone.
My head to a candle. Poof.

Poof the rags caught, ropes of flame
traveling with little giggles
and thrills, farther and farther up.
I wait for the roof to fall in.

Bleeding Ulcer

bursting into flower. Disco hibiscus
white white with a bright red core.
This is not what it looks like. Flashed
up on a screen, a snake in my entrails.
And what are entrails anyway but purple
knight delphinium turned inside out.
Too much time imagining a garden, trying
to find places inside myself for flowers,
transplanting what I know into what I don't,
into what's eating me from the inside.
Foxglove, dianthus, veronica—that shares
its name with a sewer rat, holy or otherwise.
The rat inside nibbling to get free.
What is it in the gut that wants
to escape, ride the acid high, and
there's only one way out. Black stool
as in dried blood, as in black plague,
not knowing. For days drawing over
and over the familiar face, a string
of bleeding hearts rooted in my mouth.

21 IS NOT A CLUB

I play the tourist beret, you play the brain;
you play it up—needing so many hats.
Some lovers understand the fable of indifference:
The fox doesn't care about the grapes
and they fall on his head. The saucers
stack up in my dream of France
as in all dreams. I place you there
across the street where I can examine you
as you look for me. I have a fantasy
about the fantasy of one true love—
the one we can't get back
and always want to, live our lives to,
lie to our lovers to. Even when it was real,
in the first throes of romance
it was already wrong. (All at once
the veal is served.) We make it fantastic
to make it last. It lasts too long.
We glisten our lips for sex,
all the men and women waiting—
I wonder if there's been an orgasm
in the house for the last three acts.

II

ROAD

AMERICAN BANDSTAND

I.

Objects take on the urgency of events.
Each time we stop, women caress
their fingers, examine red flicks of nail.
Beside the river vines pencil, light rain
glazes our foreheads. We promise eventually
to focus on something, but all we think of
is how much we've already borne.

II.

Maybe we could change the color of the car,
do the Philly Dog, or something calmer:
Mashed Potato, Stroll, Locomotion.

III.

Every clown has a dog named Joey
and a papier mache mask—goose, dolphin,
flame—to catch the queen. Each face
is smeared by huge diamond tears.
Mouths turn down like so many lost—
not opportunities—clocks, cocks,
socks. An army of clowns and Hugo
Zacchini, the Human Projectile.

IV.

The end of the century,
like the end of anything,
is a transportation nightmare—
every road turns back on itself,
a nation of hovering cloverleaves.
Darling, tell me there's a line out,
a new dance where you don't need
a partner, the steps are easy,
and no one waves from the mouth of a cannon.

Suite for Three Left Hands

First Hand

I change my shirt at a roadside rest, exposing
breasts to gunmetal stalls. Dying light tumbles.
Morning to dusk I drive, collecting information:
scarlet mitten, fallen leaf, four-color map of Utah.
I'm on tour with a wolfhound. Direct me
to the loneliest town in America.

Second Hand

Give up your tiredness to Santa Rosa,
New Mexico, where smoke bowls whirl
from all six of a train's engines
and a truck full of onions motors
on a parallel highway. Go I know not
where in search of I know not what.
East of Albuquerque the moon rises flat.

I track turning points, the instant
life becomes memory, but it's always beyond
my grasp. At Fort Dix, New Jersey, a man walked
on the moon. Anxious recruits watched in
black & white imagining themselves from the air
as green dots rolling across a game board.
I'd like to lead my own life for a change
but not in this neighborhood.

THIRD HAND

At the zoo white-cheeked gibbons
sing duets, waking the neighbors.
They sing to reinforce family bonds.
They sing before grooming, before
eating green beans, before hanging
off the wire of their cages.

They sing to prove nothing all happens
at once—the same way on certain days
you're trapped on the set of *This Is
Your Life* and can't get off, the green
bottle of dreams spilling its contents
over and over, a wild dog video loop.

CODA

It rains on the house of soap.

CARTOGRAPHY

Someone once slit his wrist to draw
the world for me Instead he drew it
from me or me from it
and I think the lesson here may be
never to accept sketches from strangers
no matter how attractive they appear
either the sketches or the strangers

Living with someone else's ghosts
even those accepted naively
even in the name of love
is more extreme than living
with someone else Too many adjustments
distend the spirit and the body
The drawing escapes the original artist
the original artist escapes

To a White Crow

for Bill Means

Your sheeted body rolls into mustard light,
a shot zooms in—three ribbons wrap the corpse,
detail to prove you always had
a flair for dressing. There is no sense to
the serial relationships of death—
ten thousand people in an earthquake,
you in traveling get-up: two valises,
boxes of films scripts cameras, ready
to go and go in a car you call The Honey Pig.
I see your image in motion, scenes played
too fast. Describe again the sound
your body made when it fell.

Set up a tripod then rush to stand by the marquee—
New Year Means Here We Go Again.
My breath catches your collar but is only water.
This time you've gone too far
on speed. In the mirror I come up behind you.
That's *my* head swathed in a white towel.

Every memory I have of you
takes place November 29th: two years, two cities,
one half-developed child on a Pennsylvania mountainside.
All that last night clenching the cold,
the yellow light, ladder poised against the house,
cerulean sky. I climb to hear you laugh and say,
After the first bite, space is delicious.

KUTUZOVSKY PROSPECT

Moscow 1970

In another part of the city, Mayakovsky's statue is surrounded by writers. The one I look for is not there. Across Kutuzovsky, where I live, a construction site—mountains of mud straddled by beams so cold if a worker touched one with a bare hand he'd be stuck forever. Around him comrades would gather to name their buildings—solid and useful. There are no gray hairs in Mayakovsky's soul. Bulbous clouds blow themselves out on clean streets, onto concrete tended by widows three wars old, women in layers. On Kutuzvosky Prospect, at the House of Toys, all the little mothers weep for the meeting that doesn't take place.

MARINA

There is a Poem of the End
        and it is this one
to your family—three heads on a bone—
        written in blood, pocketed.
A fleur-de-lis on the cover,
        inside swallows fly to another existence.
No one constructs the image
        of you to love. We are all up short
to your tree of bitter cups.
        Your house has glass floors—
escape impossible, the floors are carpeted
        with dry leaves. For you,
my creature of rain, seek angels
        and find men.

NATIONALISM

I think of you as a German expressionist
smashing a skeleton against the wall
accompanied by the cacophony of a thousand wind chimes.

Is this the residue of romance or have I got it
wrong? I could have sworn
there was a time we walked nightly
arm in arm: a snow-blown bridge,
icy Moskva, flag-wrapped occasions.
Or was it your credos tightly wrapped
and me influenced by them.
How could you have convinced me of so much
knowing so little?

One can only be swayed from loyalty for so long
if love constitutes destruction.

15 years later your face
leers up at me from possibility.
I've seen you all over the world.
I have seen you and I shall never see you
again—except simply.

The blind lament of *Mitternachtlieder* calls you
back to me and you come flying
over the rotting corpses of years.
How dishonest we are to embrace.

SOPRON, HUNGARY

She walks on six small suns,
the three middle nails of each foot painted gold.
Her man waits on another bench, vaguely hysterical
for the ritual loosening of her shirt.
There is no guidebook: a language invented
to keep everyone out holds them in.
On the one hand, these lovers can prove
nothing. They do not speak
as she smooths her legs onto the chaise,
counting the extravagances of love.
(In exile only this word.) Why not
panic, hysteria, stampede for a man
remembered only as a hand fluttering?
Distance and the fear of distance, new syllables
propel themselves nine time zones
arriving deaf to their own speech.
On the other hand, a young man
balances the sun on a bicycle.

BRYCE CANYON

A chiseled model with a whippet arranges her shirt
front row amphitheater. The ranger discusses plateau whiptails.
How can you say the French will eat anything?
In a canyon full of hoodoos, bristle-cone pines
find it difficult to hold their own. Drops of rain
can't decide which river to lend themselves to,
split the difference. He says this is land with a fault,
created by erosion. Differences split us.
We beat patterns into rock, beat and believe
but lose the sense of what anything....
Furniture at this elevation juts into thin air,
the second cleanest air in America. Uplift and erosion
framed by pink cliffs, imperfect and enormous.
It is so gaudy this land. We come here
hoping to find a pinnacle, hoping,
a pinnacle on which to stand and be blessed,
and, as if into a painting of heaven, cheaply ascend.

III

WHO ELSE STAYED HERE

INSOMNIA MINOR

These relatives. These women. Dead and still demanding
attention to detail. I wear their clothes—
sprigs of mountain laurel or columbine lace.
They plant my feet in soil transported,
my movements change as they assume me.
Go, they say, in and out by the same door
for the health of your soul.

A girl believes in the stone building she sees,
its moist walls, its woman who explains
why she can never marry.
You must not violate the memories of the dead.
The body of the girl's brother hangs from the ceiling.

You women, who stepped through life as if it were ....
I throw white flour from windows.

PASTORAL

No one's ever called me anything but Catalina:
I turn around to see the sky in red madness,

what I feed into it, it feeds back
and back until I am the smallest mote

in a bobcat's eye. My dog lies long
and everything I have to say is a spring,

the clack of a windy kite. I'm in love
with Peter Lorre from the Carpathian Mountains—

focused, hard-boiled eyes and nasal whine
pursued through life by himself

as a child murderer. The horizon dips and slides,
rain curtains Baboquivari.

I brought my score so I can rehearse:
Here is the time lost in the house that Fritz built.

Here is the tomb, the house that Fritz built.
What happens to the person

who owns something of yours next, like a book,
what happens to her after she owns your book?

My dog is distracted by air. I wear red shoes
and a touch of glitter on my eyelids

to help me find where everybody is these days.
My friends have disappeared into air,

I'm too fragmented they say, waiting
for the other shoe to drop,

for another man's wife to kill herself
as soon as he touches me. The landlady drives by

checking up, old bitch, heated to flame by her own greed,
jealous of my reputation, she calls too

even though I tell her she can't reach me by phone,
I'm on jury duty, busy. The bus window reflects

the rope of my days and this moment only.
My love insinuates his way under my skin

like green wood smoke, caresses my odd legs,
reminds me of the one naked line I know.

DISCORD SPEAKS ABOUT HELEN

Autumn bites in, smelling of an old arbor.
To forget the murders I have been part of
I trust the value of dreams,

especially when I am both myself and the dream
devouring me, or a gourd split open and divided.
A woman's body soaked with rain

is discovered in the woods. She wears
a plastic bag over her head. I hear leaves
crackle like small fires, cats' eyes.

In the future I will pray in a church at Kolomonskoe,
the one whose dome is strung with granite pearls.
Bozhe moi. Bozhe moi. Helen's husband says

no guilt goes around. Helen says because of me
she is born century after century, her punishment
to be seduced by men who will betray her.

Inside each of us is a broken watermelon—
sweet red pulp, slippery seeds
and shards of pale green resurfacing.

Glamorous Helen in a lambskin hat swallows
valium, Tylenol, a bottle of scotch
and repeats this scenario lifetime after life,

always near water. She said her voyage to Egypt
was rumor, a child who gets a hard on
spanking his friends. Go to the devil's

own mother in hell. Find the split end
of our conversation, so I can ask her
one last time how passion trickles

into and out of with the ease of sand
through the hourglass. I am busier than ever
these days. Nevertheless, I have my regrets.

Postcard: Widow on Her Second Honeymoon

She explains the relationship from day to day
exists to mean something, is beginning

to develop. Before her rebirth, an active woman,
she had already turned the right margin.

The setting noted on the photograph tells
and shows a miracle, once in a lifetime

over her shoulder. As love's poet
she has enthusiastic news: Adjacent to other vacations

she experiences no nostalgia for the romantic,
although not neglected the kiss the touch the breast,

or age changes the feeling on a Florida beach.
As her star has risen, nowhere a sign of defeat.

FROM A HOSPITAL BED DOWNTOWN

Give me the heat over Tucson, Arizona.
Give me no choice but not this bed,
not this roommate Amelia, dying so loudly
I cannot sleep, this final hex on my wild life.
Put down the phone, Amelia, no one's there,
and no one here speaks Portuguese,
especially at such an hour as this is,
possibly of your death, or mine,
especially if your husband were mine,
calling you back, picking at you like some kind of monkey
idly cleaning its young, and all those old women
head to toe in black and wrinkles and tears
as if some kinds of mirrors, as if looking ahead.
Making you sit up, Amelia, so you cry out,
spilling shit. Get some dignity if I have to look at you.
Fold your hands, don't flap them
like a wound up crucifix. They'll call the priest again
and your feet will stick out and he'll touch them.
I'm lying here quietly, Amelia, so you'll get the hint,
lower the octave. You're no kind of crow
and I'm no kind of sparrow. Strangers, Amelia,
is what we are, with no control over anything.

DEAR MARY

There are some days you just have to smoke candy cigarettes. I have
          a pack here my friend Ann gave me—
Tareytons, manufactured by the Stark Candy Company in Thibodaux,
          Louisiana. You wouldn't want to eat too many
but you can smoke the same one for a half hour or so. That's what
          I'm doing, moving the cigarette from side to side
in my mouth. Doesn't taste like much: bicarbonate
          of soda accounts for the grittiness.
There's an ant hill outside my house that's two feet in diameter
          and I can't tell how deep.
I thought about pouring boiling water into it to see
          what would happen.
Did you ever read about some kind of Christians, I think,
          pouring boiling oil into heretics' ears?
Maybe they weren't Christians, but the point is, torture
          is as inventive as we get.
Today on the news was a woman who felt bonded
          to a female lobster named Oscar.
This woman's kept it alive in a fish store aquarium for over a year
          as an animal rights project
even though she was going to eat the lobster for dinner
          last Valentine's day.
But they looked at each other in that moment before Oscar hit the pot
          and it's been touch and go ever since.
My neighbor, the dealer, cleans the lobster tanks at Lucky,
          the grocery. One morning
at six o'clock he was outside my house picking through stones,
          singing *I know what I'm doing*
I just don't know why. Well, you don't have to be high
          to understand that.
So I thought I should write you to kind of introduce myself
          since John and I
are getting married next month, and I hope to meet
          you sometime soon.

MEAT COUNTER IN WINTER

27 years you picked me up after work, waiting
                    outside in the Chevy.
When we stopped at Donut's Bar I'd stare at the pigs' feet
                    floating in brine while you
had a shot and a beer. They hypnotized me
                    those little pickled hooves
hanging there like they wanted bodies. I'd wait
                    for you to sneer:
You dumb Slovaks are all alike, making up things
                    that ain't going to happen.
You been at that meat counter too long, smells
                    affecting your brain.
You and your sisters—all loony. But I knew
                    Margaret was the only one
who really drove you crazy, her complaining about Frank
                    playing the numbers
with no money for good soup bones. All those years
                    when I took off
that bloody apron I knew you'd be sitting in the car
                    reading the sports page, half asleep.
Tonight I drove alone in the dark, went out for wool.
                    You know those slippers I've been knitting,
the ones with patterned blocks, they stretch to fit
                    your feet, little cushions?
It was the middle of a pattern and nobody was around.
                    I give those slippers as presents.
These are small, tan and red. I haven't decided yet
                    who they're for, but so far
I've made 32 pairs.

SHORTHAND DIARY

> "I can't bear it when lamplight struggles with daylight;
> everything seems then at its worst, I think."
> —*The Diary of Dostoyevsky's Wife*

How can I be Fyodor's one and only little wife?
As if the man could be contained or I contain
enough to satisfy one of us. A lime tree

blooms in Berlin. Through its leaves I see a dog
pull a cart piled high with milk cans,
delivering to many-storied homes on the avenue.

I reside in hotels, rooms where I bray cod liver oil
with apple jelly, hold the spoon while Fyodor laps.
If we quarrel he wakes with rheumatism, the flesh

of his left cheek a rotting pear. When will he get
the idea of winning out of his head! Like a peacock
he struts his dilapidated tail through the courtyard.

A fool, I pawn my fur coat to cover his losses,
then read his mail from Polina Suslova, the bigger fool.
She writes clumsily and brings anger

to my face in red spots. We eat pink ices
at the Hotel Victoria. I massage my husband's
calves, his thighs, anything to keep him

from the tables. Fyodor is on his knees begging
for gold pieces. I strive to be shrill.
He has lost his watch, his wedding ring.

Dresden is a town of the ugliest people,
nasty with big noses. They sell oranges
or candles. From the train I see a castle

whorled in mist, the flowers of acacia
to melt in my hand. I put a five pound note
on *Impair* and lose—cursing myself,

roulette, everything in the world. Now Fyodor
is in a minor key, now blesses me
as the darling of his heart. A little

way from town the chestnuts are rose colored,
the men walk backward on a stone path.
It is impossible to know what that means.

IV

TRYING TO BE HOME

MORNING

I live in a town that's a mango tree
dark leaves, pulpy fruit. Each morning
seven trash men sing it awake.
You can hear them from Anacostia
to Chevy Chase, not one
can carry a tune. The residents
of the Wisconsin Avenue nursing home
blink their eyes open
for that first shot of sun,
and it's their lucky day
because there is one.

                           Honey on his tongue,
Ralph Johnson licks the window glass
to lap up all of the yellow he can.
But the shift is changing
and out in the parking lot
night attendants throw off demeanor,
whoop up the neighborhood.
At 7:30 in the morning
it feels good to honk at the day.
Volume tastes like magic.

Johnson plucks an errant hair from his eye:
                Wheel me to the moon
                Where I can play among the farts.
                Let me see what life is like
                With all my working parts.
Across the street at G. C. Murphy
another fern hits the sidewalk,
smelling just like Sunday.

A thin drizzle of belief
leads him to the pavement
in his coat checkered with oatmeal.
He hopes for an audience, for me,
to ask him what Mr. Big News Channel
thinks about politics, and he'll swear
we ought to throw out the bunch
because they steal from their friends.
Hace mucho calor, Reina, in Spain.

I could call Ralph Johnson my father,
although he's not, today wearing a white Panama
with a gold crown glued to the band.
King of the Sidewalk, his deflating balloon
trails behind his wheelchair
like all the plans he, and I, ever had
for my childhood, now dragging small
behind an old man in a paper hat.

Sparkman & Water

Shorty spins down the street putting the planets in order,
praying for ash to fill his lonely gullet.

Cause and effect tells me
any number of frank dry sunrises can't erase this place.
Eight p.m.'s searing meat and desiccated orange
are the Water Street:

It is given we can't leave
against a foreign background defined.
So we make weather instead, or food—

Or what I do tonight:
create a satyr from man, goat, and Crazy Glue,
take life back into the drawing board.
I have never been able to give up the notion

that this minute will also be the next.
Shorty spins back crooning *Vegetabolic is the word for this,*
my friend, because Saturn can't live in this mess,
and that man you're making will be no better than the one you got.

So we pull up the stoop, Shorty and I,
and fasten cement to our backs, knowing that
from any crooked moment
we can watch spider flowers open on the moon.

* * *

There was a moment when we looked at each other
and said, *Yes,* said nothing is changing hands.
Crust hardens on the night and we all grow
thin. The handcuffs snapping onto two dealers across the street
further emaciate us. Shorty switches to scotch.
Mercy is no mercy, Sugar,
you eat pain now, or you eat it later.

The burned-out house on Florida camouflages
animal sacrifice. I tell Shorty
the child inside me can't open its left eye
and he says *What happens is, we forget.*

On the moon, buds spin into webs and I find the man
I lost. It comes to me that the only similarity
between where he and I live is craters.

Shorty's dark hand pulls back my thoughts
and passes me the bottle. Gibberish whirls on my tongue
as I ask why we call this home.

ACCIDENT

Jeannette, whose name I don't know, is leaving me alone in this city.
The torch and all that's left are burned pillars
how two people balled up in the flames of an oil tanker
whose driver was sleeping or maybe not. Three men
put themselves out in the dirt while Jeannette
remained in the ditch, or writhed or screamed or other
impossibilities unless you've been a human torch,
Jeanne d'Arc, another spark of possibility lighting
the fires of armies. In this case commuters, rubbernecking
and angry at six thirty in the morning, to see that fireball
Jeannette rise up to greet the day, resplendent,
winged, cursing them, inconvenient.

AMMONITE: HEMATIZED MOROCCO

The ammonite appears third hour in line
at the Bureau of Motor Vehicles
after I've exhausted all the words
about rain and it's morning again.

I give a wide berth to the woman
beside me, everyone coughs up the past
as it becomes necessary. Clambering
through any ocean one hundred

seventy million years ago
the ammonite constructed its living
chamber one secretion after the next.
Another Ho Hum Motel,

a lover's question—
Have you come to terms with
how much absence? Air in D.C.
allows no room for storage.

This is city as hologram,
nowhere to ground, central
points vanishing. The same way
the courtyard of every French

restaurant is comfortable,
the snail filled its chambers
with air to propel itself.
The woman smiles into the Polaroid

registering herself into the
decade. Those who pursue us
find another city, hair
knotted with sweat, phone lines

thick with distance. At this juncture
it's the juncture we worry about,
that—and mobility is no longer
its own reward.

River of Shoes

Like lavender sachet, they evoke the cold musk
of a great aunt's attic explored
on a day when snow blows itself into tunnels.
As you open the trunk, a wedding dress

and satin pumps time-warp into
an action where some parts of the garden
are so deeply in shade they are caves
you crawl into. Someone has left a tiny slipper,

the fairy Larkspur perhaps,
who presides over children's footwear—
sneakers, Mary Janes, bluchers—
and that is how these are, iced with dust

and faded, each shoe playing for a song.
You are alone, standing on the metal bridge
that crosses the River of Shoes:
tuning up your ear to hear a single note

or the story each shoe sings.
Who listens to a witness becomes a witness.
A bast sandal kicks up clouds in a sky
And you ask—

What were they saving them for?
The moist warmth of wool socks,
the soft pressure of an instep,
the pulse through an ankle waltzing?

Holocaust Museum
Washington, D.C.

NATIONAL CATHEDRAL

Evening
Spires as trees, this forest.
A giant sperm flashes across the horizon,
its blue tail disappearing north.

Many hands are needed to wring
as the winged horse
takes off for heaven.

Morning
Echoes from the service
male voice rhythms
and on the tapestry a spear,

perhaps a pharisee driven.
Drawn to colored glass bulbs
I fire them all.

So easy, angels,
with your blue and red wings
and all those harps wrought

in crosses and invasion.
The window of heaven,
the window of pain.

Who has the sword?
Who is running away?

Dance in the Bishop's Garden

Under her top hat, flowers,
full and transparent words.
Fur cuffs drape the wall.

She laces the veins
in her legs and stretches.
A stranger's foot

intrudes the frame.
Trousers loosely hung
spin off their axis.

SHOPPING: THE LIPSTICK CHANNEL

> *"...all I ever learned from love*
> *is how to shoot at someone who outdrew you."*
> —Leonard Cohen

What is it about the body that gets hungry at four
in the afternoon, or tired? A woman with fricasseed hair
lounges at Roma, a clothing store in Georgetown.
She wears a short skirt, a jacket with gold epaulets

and a halter top, so when she lifts herself up
from the chair, she is an angel, weightless. Only
when she walks do her hips gain mass,
commanding your eyes to follow them.

As you step down the street trying to be her
you think how your lips will, after supper,
circle a fat penis, but this time it will be slow
and you will enjoy it, watching the waxy red

transfer form a perfect kiss. Two pairs of lips,
then three until you have to excuse yourself
to freshen your lipstick. His penis and your mouth
the same shade of Cobra Red. Talk to me, baby,

he says, and all you can come up with is a recipe
for bean dip that you and Ann concocted years ago
when every afternoon you watched *Star Trek* and drank
Bohemia beer. Maybe if you had talked to her better

she would still have conversations with you rather than
silence. You have learned that it is important
to keep people, especially lovers, entertained.
The sun is hot and dangerous and feels good. Time

evaporates in it, and after a while you fall asleep
to see the woman walking toward you out of a mirror.
The crowds on M Street close in, but you don't notice
as you head for the moment where reality and

fantasy mingle, and you feel strong enough
to slip into her body, make those lips your own,
those hips obey, and croon in your huskiest voice,
Sing to me, Leonard Cohen. Sing Hallelujah!

NOTES

"Door to the River" takes its title from a Willem de Kooning painting.

"House on Fire" takes its title from a steel pipe and propane sculpture by Helen Lessick.

"Shorthand Diary"—The epigraph is from *The Diary of Dostoyevsky's Wife* translated by Madge Pemberton, The Macmillan Company, 1928.

"River of Shoes"—"Who listens to a witness becomes a witness" is a quote from Terrence des Pres.

Karen Fish

Nancy Johnson grew up in Bethlehem, Pennsylvania. She has held a variety of jobs including life guard in the Poconos, nanny in the former Soviet Union, radio and television journalist, and high school and college English teacher. She studied writing at the Writing Seminars, Johns Hopkins University and at the University of Arizona. She lives in Washington, D.C., with her husband and son.

The White Pine Press Poetry Prize

The White Pine Press Poetry Prize, established in 1995, offers a cash award of $500 plus publication of the winning manuscript. Manuscripts are accepted between September 1 and December 15 each year. The winning manuscript, which is selected by a poet of national stature, is announced the following spring, with publication following in the fall. Please write or telephone White Pine Press at 716/672-5743 for additional details.

1995   *Zoo & Cathedral* by Nancy Johnson
        Selected by David St. John

WHITE PINE PRESS

White Pine Press is a non-profit publishing house dedicated to enriching literary heritage; promoting cultural awareness, understanding, and respect; and, through literature, addressing social and human rights issues. This mission is accomplished by discovering, producing, and marketing to a diverse circle of readers exceptional works of poetry, fiction, non-fiction, and literature in translation from around the world. Through White Pine Press, authors' voices reach out across cultural, ethnic, and gender boundaries to educate and to entertain.

To insure that these voices are heard as widely as possible, White Pine Press arranges author reading tours and speaking engagements at various colleges, universities, organizations, and bookstores throughout the country. White Pine Press works with colleges and public schools to enrich curricula and promotes discussion in the media. Through these efforts, literature extends beyond the books to make a difference in a rapidly changing world.

As a non-profit organization, White Pine Press depends on support from individuals, foundations, and government agencies to bring you this literature that matters — work that might not be published by profit-driven publishing houses. Our grateful thanks to all the individuals who support this effort and to the following foundations and government agencies: Amter Foundation, Ford Foundation, Korean Culture and Arts Foundation, Lannan Foundation, Lila Wallace-Reader's Digest Fund, Margaret L. Wendt Foundation, Mellon Foundation, National Endowment for the Arts, New York State Council on the Arts, Trubar Foundation, Witter Bynner Foundation, and the Slovenian Ministry of Culture.

Please support White Pine Press' efforts to present voices that promote cultural awareness and increase understanding and respect among diverse populations of the world. Tax-deductible donations can be made to:

White Pine Press
10 Village Square · Fredonia, NY 14063

AMERICAN POETRY FROM WHITE PINE PRESS

Certainty
David Romtvedt
ISBN 1-877727-59-8   96 pages $12.00 paper

Destination Zero
Sam Hamill
ISBN 1-877727-53-9 $15.00 paper

Leaving Egypt
Gene Zeiger
ISBN 1-877727-50-4   96 pages $12.00 paper

Clans of Many Nations
Peter Blue Cloud
ISBN 1-877727-47-4   176 paghes $14.00 paper

Heartbeat Geography
John Brandi
ISBN 1-877727-40-7   256 pages $15.00 paper

Watch Fire
Christopher Merrill
ISBN 1-877727-43-1   192 pages $14.00 paper

Between Two Rivers
Maurice Kenny
ISBN 0-934834-73-7   168 pages $12.00 paper

Tekonwatonti: Molly Brant
Maurice Kenny
ISBN 1-877727-20-2   209 pages $12.00 paper

Drinking the Tin Cup Dry
William Kloefkorn
ISBN 0-934834-94-6   87 pages $8.00 paper

Going Out, Coming Back
William Kloefkorn
ISBN 1-877727-29-6   96 pages $11.00 paper

Jumping Out of Bed
Robert Bly
ISBN 0-934834-08-3   48 pages $7.00 paper

Poetry: Ecology of the Soul
Joel Oppenheimer
ISBN 0-934834-36-9   114 pages $7.50 paper

Why Not
Joel Oppenheimer
ISBN 0-934834-32-6   46 pages $7.00 paper

Two Citizens
James Wright
ISBN 0-934834-22-9   48 pages $8.00 paper

Essays About Poetry

Where the Angels Come Toward Us
David St. John
ISBN 1-877727-46-6   256 pages $15.00 paper

POETRY IN TRANSLATION FROM WHITE PINE PRESS

The Four Questions of Melancholy
Poems by Tomaz Salamun
ISBN 1-877727-57-1   224 pages $15.00 paper

These Are Not Sweet Girls
An Anthology of Poetry by Latin American Women
ISBN 1-877727-38-5   368 pages $17.00 paper

Anxious Moments
Prose Poems by Ales Debeljak
ISBN 1-877727-35-0   78 pages $12.00 paper

A Gabriela Mistral Reader
ISBN 1-877727-18-0   277 pages $13.00 paper

Alfonsina Storni: Selected Poems
ISBN 0-934834-16-4   72 pages $8.00 paper

Circles of Madness: Mothers of the Plaza de Mayo
Marjorie Agosín
ISBN 1-877727-17-2   128 pages $13.00 paper

Sargasso
Marjorie Agosín
ISBN 1-877727-27-X   92 pages $12.00 paper

Maremoto/Seaquake
Pablo Neruda
ISBN 1-877727-32-6   64 pages $9.00 paper

The Stones of Chile
Pablo Neruda
ISBN 0-934834-01-6   98 pages $10.00 paper

Vertical Poetry: Recent Poems by Roberto Juarroz
ISBN 1-877727-08-3   118 pages $11.00 paper

Light and Shadows
Juan Ramon Jimenez
ISBN 0-934834-72-5   70 pages $9.00

Elemental Poems
Tommy Olofsson
ISBN 1-877727-13-X   136 pages $12.00 paper

Four Swedish Poets: Strom, Espmark, Transtromer, Sjogren
ISBN 0-934834-97-0   140 pagers $10.00 paper

Night Open
Rolf Jacobsen
ISBN 1-877727-33-4   221 pages $15.00 paper

Selected Poems of Olav Hauge
ISBN 1-877727-03-2   92 pages $9.00 paper

Tangled Hair
Love Poems of Yosano Akiko
ISBN 0-934834-05-9   48 pages $7.50

A Drifting Boat
An Anthology of Chinese Zen Poetry
ISBN 1-877727-37-7   200 pages $15.00 paper

Between the Floating Mist
Poems of Ryokan
ISBN 1-877800-01-5   88 pages $12.00 paper